This book is a gift for

....

From

....

On this date

....

Give thanks to the Lord
because he is good.

PSALM 136:1

For my God, who truly is always good.

For Jeff and Lauren and Kaler, who

show me His goodness every day.

Love, Mom

God Is Always Good

© 2014 by Tommy Nelson

Written by Tama Fortner

Illustrated by Veronica Vasylenko

Published in Nashville, Tennessee, by Tommy Nelson. Tommy Nelson is an imprint of Thomas Nelson. Thomas Nelson is a trademark of HarperCollins Christian Publishing, Inc.

Tommy Nelson titles may be purchased in bulk for educational, business, fund-raising, or sales promotional use. For information, please e-mail SpecialMarkets@ThomasNelson.com.

Scripture quotations are taken from the INTERNATIONAL CHILDREN'S BIBLE®. © 1986, 1988, 1999 by Thomas Nelson. All rights reserved.

Library of Congress Cataloging-in-Publication Data is on file.

ISBN-13: 978-0-7180-1145-1

Printed in China

14 15 16 17 LEO 6 5 4 3 2 1

LEO / Heshan, China / August 2014 / PO # 9302590

God Is Always Good

Comfort for Kids Facing Grief, Worry, or Scary Times

By Tama Fortner

Illustrated by Veronica Vasylenko

Tommy NELSON®

A Division of Thomas Nelson Publishers

NASHVILLE   MEXICO CITY   RIO DE JANEIRO

Mommy, what is God like?

God is bigger than the mountains and stronger than
the seas. And even though He's big enough to hold the
whole world in His hands, He cares about you and me.
But the thing I love the most about God is that He is
always good.

The Lord is good.
NAHUM 1:7

Always?

YES, ALWAYS.

But how do you know *that He's good?*

Well, just look at this world around you and at all
the good things to see. Playful puppies that lick your
toes and bright, happy flowers that tickle your nose.
God made this world and all your favorite things because . . .

GOD MADE EVERYTHING
THAT IS GOOD.

God looked at everything
he had made, and
it was very good.

GENESIS 1:31

Did God make me too?

Oh, yes, *you* are some of His very best work!
God made you marvelous right from the start.
He put the twinkle in your eye and the happy
in your heart. He even put that freckle on your
cheek. He thinks you are amazing, and . . .

GOD HAS GOOD PLANS FOR YOU.

"I have good plans for you. I don't plan to hurt you. I plan to give you hope and a good future."

Jeremiah 29:11

"Don't worry, because I am
with you. Don't be afraid,
because I am your God.
I will make you strong
and will help you."

Isaiah 41:10

But sometimes not-so-good things happen.

Every day good things happen all over the world, but, yes, bad things happen too. And it's okay to wonder why. These hurtful things aren't part of God's plan, and they make Him sad too. Just remember that when bad things happen . . .

GOD IS THERE TO HELP YOU.

Does God make bad things happen?

No. God is perfect, but people are not. They make mistakes and choose to do things that are wrong. That's called sin, and it causes all the sadness. Some sin is hard to see. Other sin is big and terrible. It causes wars and makes enemies. When the troubles of this world start to worry you, be brave and believe this . . .

He who guards you
never sleeps.

PSALM 121:3

But sometimes I still get scared.

Everyone gets scared sometimes. There's nothing wrong with that! Just remember that God is with you, watching over you, day and night. He sees every smile and every tear. He knows your every worry and fear. God *even* counts the hairs on your head! You don't have to be afraid because . . .

GOD ALWAYS KEEPS WATCH OVER YOU.

Then where is God when bad things happen?

God is always there, right by our side. You just have to look and see Him. He's with the police and firefighters, so strong and brave. He's with the doctors and nurses and the lives they save. God sends people to help and to hug. Because when bad things happen . . .

GOD USES HIS PEOPLE TO SHOW HIS GREAT LOVE.

Do not forget to do good to others. And share with them what you have.

HEBREWS 13:16

Can I help too?

Of course, God wants you to help too! And the Bible tells you just what to do: give hugs to the lonely and food to the hungry and tell everyone all about Him. Because when you love others enough to help . . .

GOD CAN USE YOU
TO MAKE BAD THINGS
BETTER AGAIN.

Our love should not be only
words and talk. Our love must
be true love. And we should
show that love by what we do.

1 John 3:18

My God brightens the
darkness around me.

PSALM 18:28

But it's hard to love bullies and people who are mean.

Yes, it *is* hard, but God wants us to love those not-so-nice people too. Sometimes you can be a friend and teach that person what is good and true. But if it's not safe for you to be a friend, then praying is the thing to do. Because when you let God's love shine through in all you do and say . . .

GOD'S LOVE DRIVES THE DARKNESS AWAY.

[God] heals the brokenhearted. He bandages their wounds.

PSALM 147:3

It's sad when people cry and are hurting.

We always want the ones we love to be happy and healthy and smiling. So when they are not, it makes us sad and breaks our hearts. That's when it's time to turn to God and tell Him all about it. Pray for those who are hurting and sick, and then remember this: no matter how tough things may be . . .

Get Well Soon

GOD IS WITH US WHEN WE ARE HURTING.

I'm saddest of all when someone dies.

Yes, it's so very hard when the people we love die. But for those who love God, dying isn't the end. It's a wonderful new beginning! In heaven, there's no crying, no sickness or sadness because . . .

GOD MADE HEAVEN WONDERFUL.

No one has ever imagined
what God has prepared
for those who love him.

1 CORINTHIANS 2:9

Jesus Christ is the same yesterday, today, and forever.

HEBREWS 13:8

I wish things didn't have to change.
Why can't everything just stay the same?

Change is a part of this world, and not every change is good. People lose jobs, and friends move away, and families don't always stay together. Things in this world change, that's true. But here's some happy news—you can always count on God because . . .

GOD NEVER CHANGES.

Is there anything God can't do?

Well, there *are* a couple of things He can't do. He can't tell a lie, and He can't break a promise. And that's very good news for me and you!

God promises He'll always be there for you, and you can believe it's true because . . .

GOD KEEPS EVERY PROMISE HE MAKES.

What he says he will do, he does.
What he promises, he keeps.

NUMBERS 23:19

"For God loved the world so much that he gave his only Son. God gave his Son so that whoever believes in him may not be lost, but have eternal life."

JOHN 3:16

So God really is always good?

Just look at the world around you and
at all the good things to see. Sometimes
bad things happen, that's true. But lots
of good things happen too! And the
very best things happened long, long
ago when Jesus, God's very own Son,
came to save me and you because . . .

GOD IS ALWAYS GOOD!